A SWEDISH LEGACY

A DECORATIVE SWEDISH ARTS LEGACY
1700-1960

IN THE COLLECTIONS OF
THE NATIONALMUSEUM, STOCKHOLM

NATIONALMUSEUM

SCALA BOOKS

© 1998 Scala Books/
Nationalmuseum Stockholm

First published in 1998
by Scala Books
143–149 Great Portland Street
London W1N 5FB

All rights reserved

Distributed in the USA by
Antique Collectors' Club Limited
Market Street Industrial Park
Wappingers Falls
NY 12590   USA

Editor Barbro Hovstadius,
with contributions from
Micael Ernstell, Jan von Gerber
English editor Cherry Lewis
Designer Sara Robin

Printed and bound in Italy
by Artegrafica s.p.a. – Verona

ISBN 1 85759 159 3

© 1998 Photography
Nationalmuseum Stockholm:
Bodil Karlsson, Åsa Lundén,
Hans Thorwid

FRONT COVER
Table from the 1790s with a top
made from marble pieces excavated
from the Forum Romanum. On the
table is *The Firework Bow*, 1921, by
Edvard Hald, Orrefors

BACK COVER
Printed fabric *Pythagoras*, 1952, by
Sven Markelius for the NK textile
room

NB All measurements of items are
given in centimetres

CONTENTS

■ FOREWORD 7
OLLE GRANATH

■ THE DECORATIVE ART COLLECTION AND ITS HISTORY 8
BARBRO HOVSTADIUS

■ THE VASA RENAISSANCE AND CAROLINE BAROQUE 14
BARBRO HOVSTADIUS

■ THE AGE OF FREEDOM – FREDERICK I AND ROCOCO 20
BARBRO HOVSTADIUS

■ NEO-CLASSICISM – THE GUSTAVIAN ERA 36
BARBRO HOVSTADIUS

■ THE EMPIRE – THE AGE OF KARL XIV JOHAN 44
JAN VON GERBER

■ ROMANTICISM AND HISTORICISM 50
BARBRO HOVSTADIUS

■ FROM THE TURN OF THE CENTURY TO SWEDISH GRACE 56
BARBRO HOVSTADIUS

■ FROM FUNCTIONALISM TO SCANDINAVIAN DESIGN 74
BARBRO HOVSTADIUS

■ INDEX 96

Foreword

THE NATIONALMUSEUM'S COLLECTION of decorative art contains Swedish and foreign pieces from the Middle Ages up to the modern day. Parts of the collection have at various times been transferred to the Museum of Far Eastern Antiquities and the Mediterranean Museum. Today the collection is principally concerned with objects from the West, from the Renaissance onward. The emphasis in the decorative art collection falls on the Swedish objects whose design and relationship to the world around form the topic of this volume.

A number of years ago an exhibition of contemporary modern Swedish silverwork toured foreign museums under the title The Triumph of Simplicity. This label might to a great extent be applied to much of the best of Swedish decorative art from the last three hundred years, and even earlier. The simple and the functional in Swedish decorative art have their roots in a folk tradition of practical art which in turn stemmed from what the great 19th-century Swedish author Carl Jonas Love Almqvist once called the significance of Swedish poverty. Thus the idea of poverty is deftly reversed, giving us wealth. The Nationalmuseum now offers you a taste of that wealth.

Stockholm, November 1997
OLLE GRANATH
Director General

Nationalmuseum building, built in 1866 in the Italian Renaissance style. The central section of the main facade is adorned with sculptures and busts of Swedish artists and scientists.
Photo: Nationalmuseum

The Decorative Art Collection and its History

THE IDEA OF A NATIONAL MUSEUM of art following the European model appeared in the first half of the 19th century. The starting point was the national art collection, housed in the Royal Palace in Stockholm and administered under the name of the Royal Museum. It was a public museum, founded by Duke Karl, later Karl XIII, as a memorial to Gustav III, after the latter's death in 1792.

The Royal Museum's collection comprised older royal acquisitions from the time of Gustav Vasa, mainly paintings, sculptures and drawings. Using public money Gustav III purchased his parents' (Adolf Fredrik and Lovisa Ulrika's) collections with the intention of making them state property. While travelling in Italy in 1783–84 he acquired antique sculptures, both originals and copies, together with vases and bronzes. A government official named Carl Fredrik Fredenheim (1748–1803), an erudite expert on antiquity and a good administrator, was given charge of the Royal Museum. The most interesting of his successors was head curator Lars Jacob von Röök (1778–1867). In approximately 1840 he instigated a thorough refitting and reorganisation of the limited space and distributed illustrated catalogues showing the position of the pieces. The Royal Museum's collections grew in size thanks to gifts from various quarters and the premises became totally inadequate. In 1845 Parliament decided that a new museum should be built and The City of Stockholm provided the plot at Strömmen, opposite the Royal Palace. The job of designing the building went initially to the architect Fredrik Wilhelm Scholander, then to the German architect Friedrich August Stüler. His building, with its clear Venetian Renaissance influence, set the tone for the architectural developments along the waters of Strömmen.

When the Nationalmuseum opened in 1866 there was no department of decorative arts. Nor had there been one in the plans for the Royal Museum. The earlier museum had, however, contained a collection of Italian majolica, known as The Raphael China, which had been crown property since the 17th century. Röök created a porcelain room where this collection was exhibited together with Greek red-figure vases. In addition, there was some Chinese and Japanese porcelain, plus Meissen pottery and bronzes. In the new museum these pieces were included in the painting department, but were seen as the embryo of a department of applied art. The new museum had no budget for the expansion of its collections, so was wholly dependent on gifts. One of these gifts, and an important one, was a collection of faience and porcelain from Rörstrand and Marieberg potteries donated in memory of Lord Chamberlain Carl Rudolf Cederström. Three more important gifts followed leading to the establishment of a department of applied art in 1885.

The first of these was Karl XV's collection in Ulriksdal Palace bequeathed to the state in 1873. The then Crown Prince Karl XV had begun to fill this palace with older decorative art, principally

Plan of a wall display in the Porcelain Room in the Royal Museum. Watercolour by Lars Jacob von Röök, 1840. NMH 112/1979.

in renaissance and baroque styles. He was helped in this by the architect Fredrik Wilhelm Scholander. Each room was arranged around a particular original piece, bought by the King, inherited, or received as a gift. Around this central piece a homogenous setting was created, using newly made objects in period style, with contemporary technical innovations such as sprung upholstery and industrial textile weaving. On the continent historicism was the fashion in decoration for the upper echelons of society, and Karl XV introduced this fashion in Sweden. Hence his collection of around 2,500 pieces was a typical 19th-century collection, combining objects of the highest quality with more historical-romantic pieces, comprising furniture, ceramics, glass, worked metal and enamel. In 1871 the collection was catalogued by the Austrian art historian Jakob von Falke.

Collecting was very popular at this time. In the circles around the King there was a Lord Chamberlain named Axel Bielke, a passionate collector of fine and applied art. In his will in 1877 he bequeathed approximately 2,200 ceramic pieces. Half of these were from China and Japan, and are now housed in the Museum of Far Eastern Antiquities. Most of the rest came from Rörstrand and Marieberg. Some came originally from the "porcelain kitchen" in Sturefors Palace which belonged to his father, Count Gustav Ture Bielke, but most were purchases. From his notes we know that antique dealers and auctions were fruitful sources. In Sweden the property of a deceased person is often auctioned, not infrequently at the deceased's former residence. Bielke bought at these *dödsbo* auctions around Sweden; he bought at official auctions in Stockholm; he bought from sellers of antiquities Mlle Eklund and Mlle Öberg; from clothes stalls in Drottninggatan (to this day a popular shopping street in central Stockholm), and he bought from friends. He also bought while on study trips to various museums in Europe. Parts of Axel Bielke's collection were shown at an exhibition in 1876–77 in the Prince Royal's Palace (today the Ministry of Foreign Affairs) in an exhibition which aimed to highlight the need for a state museum of decorative art.

The Great Exhibition of 1851 in London had given rise to the first decorative art museum in

Karl XV's layout of the Oxenstiernska room in Ulriksdal Palace. Some of the furniture, textiles and pewter objects from the 16th and 17th centuries are among the most important objects in the museum's collection. Lithograph by Carl Johan Billmark, 1871.

the modern sense, the Museum of Manufacturers in Somerset House which later became the Victoria and Albert Museum. The idea was to have exhibits which would educate manufacturers and public alike in technical matters and in matters of taste. In the late 19th century similar museums were opened in Europe with the same aim. In Stockholm in 1872 the Swedish Society for Industrial Design had begun to set up a Museum of Industrial Arts and Crafts. The driving force behind this was Fritz von Dardel, the newly appointed president of the Society. His international contacts made him an important conduit for foreign ideas concerning the reform of industrial art. The museum collected 17th- and 18th-century Swedish and foreign decorative art and contemporary industrial production from Vienna, Prague, Moscow and elsewhere. Also Swedish industry contributed examples of its produce: wallpaper from Kåbergs, china and porcelain from Gustavsberg, iron and steel pieces from Eskilstuna Jernmanufacture AB. The textile collection included lacework from the Friends of Textile Art Association and woven fabrics from the Skåne region bought by the artist Jakob Kulle.

When the Department of Decorative Art was opened at the Nationalmuseum in 1885 it was seen as a solution to the long talked about question of a special museum for applied art. The department was housed on the middle floor of the museum and the combined collections were grouped by material in a number of arranged interiors. An article in the publication *Ny Illustrerad Tidning* praised the arrangement but lamented that the building was too modern to do justice to the material. We believe today that the red-painted walls, the pillars and the decorated arches set off the renaissance and baroque pieces well, though the later periods are more difficult to harmonise.

The first head of this department was Ludvig Looström who had been amanuensis at the

Renaissance room with Erik Folker's new layout, 1925.

museum of the Society for Industrial Design. In 1900 Looström was made Director of the Nationalmuseum and a successor was not appointed until 1913, when Gustav Folker was given the post. He decided that the display was antiquated and planned a complete reorganisation. In 1919 he became Director so the work was implemented by his successor, Erik Wettergren. Folker believed that the pieces should not recreate a living or working space, but should be displayed according to artistic criteria. He also wanted to introduce labelling to satisfy the demand for information.

Erik Wettergren had been one of the organisers of the Exhibition of the Home of 1917. During his periods in charge, 1920–28 and 1934–46, some of the first temporary exhibitions were held: Modern French Glass and Ceramics in 1927, and Modern Finnish Rya Rugs and Tapestries in 1939. There followed a series of large exhibitions which focused on Swedish industrial art. In 1928–34 Åke Stavenow took over the position. He wrote a treatise on Carl Hårleman and took a special interest in 18th-century furniture and modern decorative and industrial art. During Carl Hernmarck's long period in charge (1946–65) there were several large exhibitions including Practical Art in 1949 and Wilhelm Kåge in 1953. He became best known for his research into older silverware and ceramics, but he also introduced design with Five Designers in 1957. Under Hernmarck the department achieved its current (physical) size. In 1966, Dag Widman of the Society for Industrial Design took over as head of the department, and rearranged the permanent collection, with the various materials integrated into the arrangement by period and style. Post-1900 works were given more space and many major exhibitions of decorative art from the 1960s and 1970s were organised. During 1981–1995 his successor Helena Dahlbäck Lutteman strengthened the focus on 20th-century

Orrefors Exhibition, 1942. One of the early exhibitions which focuses on modern Swedish industrial art.

decorative art and design, while personally specialising in the older ceramics and silverware.

Among the donations which have enriched the collection this century are notably District Judge Carl Dahlgren's collection of European boxes and pocket-watches and the wholesaler W. Bendix's glassware collection, including Swedish glassware from the 18th and early 19th centuries. Since the inception of the department, its strength has been its ceramics. The most significant gift is director Ivan Traugott's collection of 18th-century European porcelain, donated in 1950. Another area where donations have been important is silverware, most significant being a collection of late 17th- and 18th-century Swedish silverware, a gift to the museum in 1965 from company director Gunnar V. Philipson. Through the society Friends of the National Museum the museum has received gifts in all the various materials.

It is interesting to follow the connection between purchases and the major exhibitions. In 1897 the museum received a special grant to purchase from the Stockholm Exhibition, leading to the far-sighted acquisition of Swedish ceramics and textiles by Alf Wallander and Gunnar Wennerberg as well as glassware by Gallé, Leveillé and Tiffany. In the early 1900s the department received gifts of glass from Kosta Glassworks and silver from Gustav Möllenborg & Co. For the 1909 Stockholm Exhibition the "Boberg Room" was donated by two directors of Nordiska Kompaniet (NK), Josef Sachs and K.L. Lundberg. It comprised furniture and textiles designed by Ferdinand Boberg and manufactured in NK's workshops. The Baltic Exhibition of 1914 saw the purchase of Swedish textile art and stoneware, but the Exhibition of the Home in 1917, considered to be the birth of modern Swedish industrial art, brought no acquisitions at all, leaving a gap which was only filled, through

Exhibition of 20th-century decorative and industrial art, organised by Helena Dahlbäck Lutteman. Photo:1991.

purchases, much later. In 1917 there was a purchase of some of Simon Gate's new Graal glass.

In 1920 decorative art began to be acquired using a grant specially reserved for the work of living Swedish artists, which had hitherto only been used for the visual arts. It was used to acquire a clock by Carl Malmsten and an engraved bowl by Edvard Hald. Since the 1920s modern decorative art has been bought with the aim of documenting all that is new and interesting. The 1930 Stockholm Exhibition brought 20 or so purchases of individually made decorative art, but no industrially manufactured standard goods. These would not be viewed seriously until the late 1950s.

Industrial design is the third and youngest category in the department. It was in the 1950s when attention was first turned to the designers of vacuum cleaners, refrigerators, telephones and television sets. Industrial design made its breakthrough in the 1950s when these consumer goods were "signed" by well-known designers whose names became a marketing asset. There were some isolated purchases in the 1930s, but it is only in the 1970s that we see the formation of the ambition to document Swedish industrial design and its relationship to developments abroad.

The decorative art collection today comprises over 30,000 pieces. We collect and display, in both permanent and temporary exhibitions, objects from Western culture from the Renaissance to the modern day. The emphasis is on the story of Swedish work, although we place equal importance on European exhibits because of the close relationship to development in Europe. The Nationalmuseum is a museum of art and consequently the demand for artistic quality has always been fundamental, together with an endeavour to document the characteristic elements of each period.

BARBRO HOVSTADIUS

The Vasa Renaissance and Caroline Baroque

RENAISSANCE STYLE COINCIDES with the rule of the Vasa dynasty, i.e. from the 1520s to the middle of the 17th century. The new nation-state was founded with the election of Gustav Vasa as King in 1523 and the institution of a hereditary monarchy in 1544. Renaissance form was introduced primarily by German and Dutch artists and craftsmen who were active in the construction of the royal palaces. Gustav Vasa built castles and maintained a simple court, but his sons Erik XIV and Johan III created a renaissance milieu on a more continental scale. At Kalmar Castle we can study interiors from the 1560s and 1570s in Italian and Southern German Renaissance style, which became models for other royal and aristocratic palaces. Here we see the combination of international forms and simple domestic traditions, characteristic of so much Swedish art.

Furniture positioned against the walls was typical in the 16th century, but subsequently we see free-standing pieces following the foreign model. Luxuriantly inlaid chests and cabinets were the grandiose furniture of the time. Since medieval times chairs had been viewed as furniture for the nobility but in the 17th century the number of chairs increased among the commoners. Most popular were chairs in the Dutch style with straight legs, simple profiles and rectangular backs.

In order to meet demand for fine textiles, beadworkers and tapestry weavers moved from palace to palace with their workshops. The foremost weavers were Paul de Bucher who came from Flanders in 1552 and died in Sweden in 1565 and the Swede Nils Eskilsson. Only a few woven tapestries have been preserved. These include two from a series of five depicting the Nordic kings of legend, probably from drawings by Domenicus ver Wilt.

Table silver was a princely luxury that appeared in Italy during the Renaissance. We can get some idea of the royal silver from lists that have been preserved. Of the wealth constituting standing cups, dishes and bowls, only one plate and one stoup remain.

The Thirty Years' War (1618–48), in which Sweden was one of the victors, made her a major power. For provincial Sweden, German influence became strong in the fine and decorative arts, reinforced by the movement of the guilds' craftsmen. A key element was the Southern German art of intarsia, which reached Mälardalen from Lübeck, and flourished as the Västerås School.

In the reign of Karl XI (1655–97) the power of the monarchy increased, and this is known in Sweden as the Caroline Dictatorship. Swedish style followed the European baroque, and with an eye on Louis XIV's court and the Palace at Versailles the architect Nicodemus Tessin the Younger wanted to create a royal residence in grand style. To decorate and furnish the Royal Palace in Stockholm, following a fire in 1697, he enlisted French artists from the circles of Charles Le Brun. Against the richly sculpted French baroque went a restrained, almost bourgeois simplicity, which had its models in Holland and England. In 1676 the first major glassworks in Sweden, Kungsholm Glassworks, was established. The work was initially based on Venetian models, later Bohemian, and Kungsholm Glassworks became famous for its decorated goblets, rummers and decanters.

BARBRO HOVSTADIUS

Tapestry, *Venusbrunnen (The Well of Venus)*, mid 16th century
Wool, silk and gold thread
Paul de Bucher (d. 1565)
191 x 420
NMK 124/1892
Gift, 1892

When the Renaissance broke through in the 1530s in the Flemish tapestry workshops it heralded the introduction of perspective compositions with classical figures of antiquity. Here, a garden landscape opens out towards a distant horizon. Wide borders ornamented with grotesques, flowers and fruit frame the subject like a painting.

Detail with the coat of arms of the Vasa dynasty woven into the centre of the upper border.

Stoup, beginning of 17th century
Silver, partly gilded
Unknown master
H 17
NMK CXV 36
Bequeathed by Karl XV, 1872

An inscription on the lid, plus the gilded coat of arms shows that this stoup belonged to Duke Johan of Östergötland (1589-1618), son of Johan III and Gunilla Bielke. The low, compact form was the norm during the baroque and rococo periods.

Cups, 1693, 1701, 1705
Silver, partly gilded
Henning Petri, 1693, master in Nyköping 1657–1702
H 17
NMK 37/1965
Gift from Friends of the Nationalmuseum, 1965

Johan Nützel, 1701, master in Stockholm 1674–1716
H 18
NMK 58/1977
Gift, 1977

Abraham Trautzell, 1705, master in Stockholm 1700–10
H 18.5
NMK 105/1968
Gift, 1968

These Caroline cups with their straight, smooth bodies that rise in a cone shape are a Swedish expression of Anglo-Dutch bourgeois simplicity.

Candlesticks, 1690
Pewter
Johan Johansson, master in Stockholm 1677–1715
H 11.5
Dep. Armoury

Pewter services for the court of Queen Hedvig Eleonora (1636–1715) at the Palaces of Gripsholm, Strömsholm, Svartsjö, and Vadstena were decorated with her crowned monogram HERS and the name of the palace. The plate and the cup take their form from the 16th century whereas the candlesticks belong to the Caroline baroque of the late 17th century.

Plate, 1668
Pewter
Unmarked
D 25.5
NMK CXV 1982
Bequeathed by Karl XV, 1872

Cup, 1668
Pewter
Vieth Fijtsson Drenchler, master in Stockholm 1637–84
H 18.5
NMK CXV 1980
Bequeathed by Karl XV, 1872

Goblets with Covers, 1680s
Glass
Kungsholm Glassworks, Stockholm
H 43 and H 31
NMK CXV 183
NMK CXV 1701
Bequeathed by Karl XV, 1872

These goblets both have a thin, blown bowl standing on a monogrammed stem, an object type which is seen as Swedish even if isolated examples appear elsewhere. The combined monogram of the royal couple Karl XI and Ulrika Eleonora is shaped in glass thread. One theory is that this was first produced for their wedding in 1680.

Credence Tray with Glass and Carafe, c. 1700
Glass
Kungsholm Glassworks, Stockholm
H 9.8 (tray), H 6 (glass), and H 16.5 (carafe)
NMK 26/1890
NMX 181
Purchase, 1890

Kristoffer Elstermann introduced the art of engraving to the glassworks in the 1690s. Many of the motifs were brought from the continent and were then used by the glassworks' engravers long into the 18th century. On this carafe, a typical form from this glassworks, a sprinkling of flowers is evident.

The Age of Freedom – Frederick I and Rococo

The label 'Age of Freedom' refers to the political freedom which reigned after the end of the Caroline dictatorship, lasting from the death of Karl XII in 1718 until the revolution of Gustav III in 1772. At this time power lay with the Council and Parliament. In 1720 Fredrik I, who was married to Karl XII's sister Ulrika Eleonora, became Regent. He was succeeded in 1751 by Adolf Fredrik of Holstein-Gottorp, husband of Lovisa Ulrika, sister of Fredrik II of Prussia.

The most important event in the world of art was the resumption of the construction of the Royal Palace of Stockholm in 1727. Work was led by Superintendent Carl Gustav Tessin (1695–1770) and Court Intendant Carl Hårleman (1700–53). Under Hårleman's leadership Jean Eric Rehn (1717–93) was responsible for furniture and interiors. When the court moved into the palace in 1754 the work was not finished, and it continued into the 1770s under the leadership of Carl Johan Cronstedt (1709–77) and Carl Fredrik Adelcrantz (1716–96).

The breakthrough of rococo in Sweden is bound up with the construction of the palace and its artistic direction. It was Hårleman and Rehn who, taking French rococo as a starting point, gave the style its restrained Swedish character. French artists were brought in during the period from 1732 and examples of furniture, textiles, chandeliers, etc. were imported from the French. In the workshops of the palace Swedish artists and craftsmen were educated in the rococo style, which began to reach Swedish homes in the 1750s, but only made a real impact in the 1760s.

During the Age of Freedom trade and industry were keenly pursued along commercial lines. Everything manufactured in the country meant income and particularly in the case of luxury articles. A special office was set up in 1739 to support domestic production. In 1744 Jean Eric Rehn was employed there as pattern designer to the textile industry. Ten years later he travelled to France with the task of bringing back examples of both textiles and faience. The objects he brought back for the industries and craftsmen were greatly influential in shaping the Swedish rococo.

The textile industry was the most important manufacturing branch. Wool production was most common, while linen and silk were luxury goods. In Flor, in the province of Hälsingland, a linen-maker's was established in 1729 whose damask for the court and the aristocracy became famous. Silks were needed for the upper classes and the state invested heavily in silk-weaving mills. In the 1760s there were around 40 factories in Stockholm.

To achieve domestic production of porcelain and chinaware Rörstrand was set up in 1726 and Marieberg in 1758, both in Stockholm. Success did not come until the 1770s, but the faience that was made is equal in quality to contemporary production in Europe. Kosta Glassworks was established in 1741, making window glass, tableware and chandeliers. Other goods, such as furniture, silverware, clocks and watches were produced mainly by the guilds of craftsmen.

BARBRO HOVSTADIUS

Fredrik I's Burial Cup, 1751
Silver-gilt
Gustaf Stafhell the Elder, master in Stockholm 1714–55
H 31
NMK 104/1968
Gift, 1968

The cup was a gift to Archbishop Henrik Benzelius for Fredrik I's burial in 1751. The festoons of roses, laurel and grain symbolised victory, resurrection and eternal life. The wing-like ornamentation round the medal is a motif to which Carl Hårleman often returns in his work.

Chest of Drawers, 1740s
Walnut veneer
Olof Martin, master in Stockholm
1736–64
H 85
NMK 25/1985
Gift from Friends of the
Nationalmuseum, 1985

Master carpenter and guildmaster Olof Martin trained in Paris and London. The chest shows inspiration from the earlier French rococo. The Kolmården marble top was new at this time.

Miniature Tile Oven, 1746
Faience
Rörstrand Porcelain Factory, Stockholm
H 19
NMK 10/1903
Purchase, 1903

Model for the tile oven with blue and white decoration introduced by Rörstrand in the 1740s. Carl Hårleman and later Jean Eric Rehn designed the originals. The two-part oven with its protruding shelf and ridge became standard in palaces and mansions.

Dish, 1740s
Faience
Christian Precht (1706–79)
Rörstrand Porcelain Factory, Stockholm
D 48
NMK BS 2077
Bequeathed by Count Axel Bielke, 1877

The Northern Star was adopted by Karl XI as his personal emblem in the 1680s. It lived on through the whole of the 18th century as both a royal and a national symbol. The Northern Star and the borders in airy Berain style are probably designed by Christian Precht, goldsmith and pattern designer. The dish was painted by Johan Hedberg.

Table Clock, 1740s/50s

Case lined with mirror-glass, brass mechanism with moulded and engraved ornamentation, travelling case of polished oak
Stockholms Manufabrique
H 57
NMK 95/1989
Purchase, 1989

Swedish table clocks were made from the beginning of the 18th century modelled on English mantel clocks. Stockholms Manufabrique was run by watchmaker Peter Schnack (d. 1742). In 1753 control passed to Petter Ernst, the leading rococo clockmaker in Stockholm. This clock bears the number 100.

THE AGE OF FREEDOM – FREDERICK I AND ROCOCO 23

Napkin, 1750s
Damask linen
Flor Linen Mill, Flor
92 x 90
NMK 203/1932
Gift, 1932

The symmetrical crown pattern together with a border of scale patterns after foreign models was used for the coronation table linen of Adolf Fredrik and Lovisa Ulrika. The Royal table linen had a baroque character throughout the 18th century.

Boxes, 1756
Frantz Bergs, master in Stockholm
1725–77

Gold, chased and beaten decoration, inside lid mythological scene in gouache
H 2.2
NMK 68/1940
Gift, 1940

Gold, embossed and chased
H 2.4
NMK 2/1937
Purchase, 1937

Gold, enamel decoration
H 3.7
NMK 49/1992
Gift from Friends of the Nationalmuseum, 1992

The gold box was an established gift in the 18th century, a token of esteem between people of high station. Frantz Bergs, appointed court jeweller in 1742, was known for his exquisite gold boxes, both in rococo and in the new austere classicism, which broke through in France in the 1750s.

Coin and Medal Cabinet, 1750s

Walnut veneer, fire-gilded bronze mountings
Lars Nordin, master in Stockholm, 1752–73, from a design by Carl Hårleman
H 152
Royal Academy of Antiquities

The cabinet is part of a series of eight which were made for the coin chamber, the first equipped museum room in Queen Lovisa Ulrika's apartments at Drottningholm (the palace on the outskirts of Stockholm), which she received as a birthday present in 1744.

Chair, 1750s
Alder painted in gesso, upholstery embroidered in petit point with silk and wool
Stockholm
H 104
NMK 123/1979
Purchase, 1979

The chair was probably made by a chair-maker and ornamental sculptor working on the furnishing of the Royal Palace in Stockholm. The embroidery is sewn on to pre-marked patterns on material grounds imported from France. They are marked *Marchand de la Laine rue des Lombards aux Signe de la Croix*.

Interior, *Les Deux Pendules (The Two Clocks)*, 1763
Watercolour on pencil drawing
Olof Fridsberg (1728–95)
10.5 x 19.5
NMH 393/1927
Gift from Friends of the Nationalmuseum, 1927

The picture is an illustration in one of the four books of fables written by the Tessin and Sparre families as a literary pastime in the years 1757–1764. It is made up of objects which were in Count Carl Gustaf Tessin's home on the estate of Åkerö. Fridsberg the painter joined the household where he undertook book illustrations and wall paintings.

Tea Table, 1760s
Painted wood, faience tray
Rörstrand Porcelain Factory,
Stockholm
H 70, (table) and 87 x 58 (tray)
NMK 37/1888
Purchase, 1888

The table with faience tray was a
popular innovation of the period.
The deep faience tray was ideal
for ceremonies centred around
tea drinking. The lush botanical
designs on the faiences of Rörstrand
and Marieberg correspond with the
time when Carl von Linné was at
the height of his glory, a fact which
was certainly not a coincidence.

Masterpiece Cabinet, 1758
Walnut veneer, fire-gilded bronze mountings
Carl Schalin, master in Stockholm 1758–84
H 254
NMK 36/1977
Purchase, 1977

In the rococo period in Stockholm carpenters would, for their masterpiece, make a cabinet with two drawers and doors and three 'columns'. Curving S-lines and rounded corners are recurring features, but the veneer patterns and the top-pieces vary.

Wall Clock, 1750s
Casing of gilded bronze, with porcelain flowers
Eric Sundberg, court clockmaker
1746, (d. before 1765)
H 49
HMK 301/1995
Purchase, 1995

The wall clock, with its irregular rocaille forms became an element of the complete interior modelled on the French. The bronze case and the mechanism were made in Stockholm but the porcelain flowers were probably imported. The clock originally belonged to Carl Fredrik Adelcrantz. It hung in the drawing-room of his country-house in Trångsund outside Stockholm.

Chest of Drawers, 1760s
Jacaranda and plum veneers, fire-gilded bronze mountings, Öland limestone top
H 85
NMK 38/1894
Gift from Superintendent's office, by Royal letter, 1894

On this fully developed rococo-style chest of drawers the whole facade is a coordinated surface framed by decorative bronze mountings. The chest bears the owner's mark of Gustav III when Crown Prince. It was once part of the furnishings of Uppsala Palace.

Dish and Sugar Shakers, 1750s
Faience
Rörstrand Porcelain Factory, Stockholm
L 44 and H 19
NMK BS 208, 2026–27
Bequeathed by Count Axel Bielke, 1877.

With this design the rococo came to Rörstrand. It was composed by Jean Eric Rehn who studied in Paris in the 1740s. The pattern was used on all types of object for three decades after 1748. It was usually painted in blue on a blue-tinted background with white patterning, known as *bianco sopra bianco*.

Cream Jugs,
1765 and undated
Faience
H 10
Marieberg Faience Factory,
Stockholm
NMK 218
Gift, 1867

Silver, gilded on inside
Olaus Hasselquist, master in
Jönköping 1768–92
H 10.5
NMK 2095/1885
Gift from Swedish Society for
Industrial Design, 1884

These cream jugs are completely in the rococo spirit with their lobate leaves. Silver was an expensive material which, for tableware, came increasingly to be replaced by faience and porcelain.

Vase, c. 1765
Faience
Rörstrand Porcelain Factory,
Stockholm
H 36
NMK 10/1915
Purchase, 1915

Enamel colour, also called Muffle colour, made it possible to achieve a rich, natural, living decoration. The painter Erik Wahlberg, one of Rörstrand's most able, here exploits the whole range of newly achievable colours.

Tureen, 1765
Faience
Marieberg Faience Factory,
Stockholm
H 31
NMK 35/1916
Gift, 1916

Among the modellers at Marieberg in the 1760s worked Olof Årre, who had studied under the ornamental sculptor Adrien Masreliez. Årre's tureen with mussels, shells and crayfish in relief on the lid is an independent contribution to Swedish rococo faience where foreign forms dominate.

Candlestick, c. 1765
Faience
Marieberg Faience Factory,
Stockholm
H 35
NMK 46/1926
Gift from Friends of the
Nationalmuseum, 1926

The series, influenced by the style of chinoiserie, includes European figurines with Chinese ornamentation. This magnificent candlestick had as its closest inspiration the figurines of Nymphenburg. It is one of a limited number thought to have been made. The strong, clear colours were applied by Johan Otto Frantzen, the foremost painter at Marieberg.

Table Surtout, 1761
Silver, partly gilded.
Kilian Kelson, master in Stockholm
1746–71
H 36.5
NMK 119/1978
Gift, 1978

Kelson was one of the foremost rococo goldsmiths. He made at least seven examples of this object in full rococo style with energetic upward-moving spirals and decoratively chased cartouches on the bulging surfaces.

Tureen, 1773

Silver
Pehr Zethelius, master in
Stockholm 1766–1810
H 28
NMK 1/1977
Gift, 1977

The tureens follow a homogenous design with soft, smooth, rounded surfaces contrasting with moulded and chased parts. Drawings with designs for the royal table indicate that the model was French. Zethelius was the most productive goldsmith of the era, active from the rococo through to the neo-classical period.

Coffee Pot, 1774

Silver, handle of blackened wood
Simsom Ryberg, master in
Stockholm 1771–1807
H 28
NMK 32/1915
Gift, 1915

During the late rococo coffee pots of the French design, with three leaf-shaped feet and a high asymmetric lid, were made all over Sweden. The decoration runs consistently, with chased floral bouquets on the body, spout and lid.

Neo-Classicism – the Gustavian Era

At the same time as rococo was making its breakthrough in Sweden there appeared in France a new stylistic fashion inspired by classical antiquity. In France this style was named Louis Seize, after the reigning King. The same happened in Sweden where Gustav III (1746–92) was much more influential in the artistic and cultural life of the times than was Louis XVI in France. Shortly after his return from Paris and accession to the throne in 1771 Gustav had a suite of rooms at the Royal Palace in Stockholm redecorated in white and gold, with imposing columns and pilasters. It was designed by Jean Eric Rehn who led the stylistic change from rococo to Gustavian classicism. The change was effected via a return to plain surfaces, straight lines and classical details such as beadings, rosettes and garlands. Veneered furniture in light woods was richly lined but with few bronze mountings. Light and airy colours prevailed, with pearl-grey the predominant colour for furniture and fixtures. Wholly gilded console tables and chairs were set in interiors used for entertaining.

While on a trip to Italy in 1783–84 Gustav III was greatly impressed with architecture of classical antiquity. This was of decisive importance for the understanding and development of art and architecture in Sweden. The creation of a neo-classical style for the royal interiors was entrusted to Louis Masreliez (1748–1810). Funded by a royal scholarship he had carried out a thorough study of antique art in Rome. A magnificent example of his artistic skill with interiors in the Pompeiian style is Gustav III's Pavilion at Haga, completed in 1791. His style of decoration was widely adopted and, together with mahogany-veneered furniture and dark-stained chairs in the English style after the model of Hepplewhite and Sheraton, formed part of the late Gustavian style, belonging to the decades around the year 1800.

BARBRO HOVSTADIUS

Draft Design for Mineral Cabinet, 1773
Washed pencil drawing
Jean Eric Rehn (1717–93)
37.4 x 43.8
NMH 185/1892
Gift, 1892

This cabinet was intended for a collection of Swedish minerals that Gustav III wanted to present to the Prince of Bourbon-Condé who was a natural history enthusiast. It was made by Georg Haupt with richly sculpted bronzes by Adrien Masreliez. The cabinet still stands in the Palace of Chantilly outside Paris.

Canopied Bed, 1770s
Carved and gilded wood, blue
silk with silver brocade
H 145 (excl. canopy)
NMK 927/1927
Gift, 1927

This bed once stood at the Gimo Works manor house, erected in 1760 from drawings by Jean Eric Rehn. It is conceivable that Rehn also designed certain pieces of furniture. The feature of having the long side of the bed against the wall was an innovation at this time. It became common throughout the 19th century under the name Gustavian bed.

Chandelier, 1780s
Crystal glass and bronze
H 100
NMK 133/1919
Gift, 1919

At the end of the century chandeliers had more but smaller drops resembling a glittering cascade. The metal is of secondary importance though some gilded mountings were well made. The candle arms are plain and reminiscent of number fives lying on their backs. At the base the chandeliers have either drops or as here a coloured glass bowl.

Chest of Drawers, 1780
Birch and other veneers
Georg Haupt, master in Stockholm 1769–84
H 88.5
NMK 925/1927
Gift from the Friends of the
Nationalmuseum, 1927

In his decorative furniture for the Swedish court and aristocracy Haupt employed, with small variations, a neo-classical form that was entirely his own. The decoration of medallions and garlands is effected with lines reminiscent of copper-plate engraved models.

DETAIL OF THE MEDALLION
The designs for the medallions and other decorations on Haupt's furniture are thought to have been drawn by Jean Eric Rehn.

Urns with Lids, 1780s

Strömbäck Glassworks, Umeå and
Gothenburg Glassworks, Gothenburg
H 22 and H 35
NMK 103–104/1971
NMK 2/1957
Purchases, 1971 and 1957

Both the coloured glass and the shape of the urns were derived from antiquity. The cobalt blue was very popular and sometimes the urns were given a white-opal rim for contrast. Several glassworks produced blue glass, but these urns are traditionally associated with Gothenburg Glassworks.

Sugar Bowl, 1798

Silver
Simsom Ryberg, master in
Stockholm 1771–1807
H 12
NMK 69/1949
Purchase, 1949

The commissioner of this bowl in the shape of a Greek kylix must have been very familiar with the forms of antique vessels. One possibility is Carl August Ehrensvärd (1745–1800), soldier, art philosopher and designer. He made several sketches of similar pieces which were realised in silver.

Tureens with Trays,
a pair, 1793
Silver, gilded inside
Arvid Floberg, master in Stockholm
1763–1802
H 38.6
NMK 173–74/1942
Gift, 1942

These late Gustavian tureens have a pure, simple classicism, modelled on work in the catalogues which were distributed by the platers of Sheffield and Birmingham.

Coffee Pot and Sugar Bowl,
c. 1775
Porcelain
Marieberg Faience Factory, Stockholm
H 20 (pot) and H 14 (sugar bowl)
NMK 21/1896, NMK BS 2333
Purchase, 1896, bequeathed by Count Axel Bielke, 1877

With shapes borrowed from an ancient column, plus right-angled handle, stone pine cones, and laurel garlands, neo-classicism makes its entrance into tableware at Marieberg under the direction of Henrik Sten.

Coffee Pot and Sugar Box,
1799 and 1798
Silver, wooden handle on pot
Pehr Zethelius, master in Stockholm 1766–1810
H 25 and H 17
NMK, 106–107/1928
Purchase, 1928

The grooved column shafts of antiquity were recurrent models in the Gustavian era. This piece belonged to Princess Sofia Albertina (1753–1829), sister of Gustav III.

Table, 1790s
Painted and gilded wood, marble top
Unmarked
H 82
NMK 107/1937
Purchase, 1937

This table, with its top made from small squares of antique marble, once belonged to Carl Fredrik Fredenheim (1748–1803), civil servant and amateur archaeologist. He carried out excavations at the Forum Romanum in 1788–89 and had several table tops made from the excavated marble. Following the death of Gustav III in 1792 he was appointed director of the royal art collections. The frame of the table was probably made by Pehr Ljung (1743–1819), one of the most skilful and frequently commissioned ornamental sculptors of the age.

Chair, c. 1800
Gilded wood, silk upholstery
Unmarked
H 78
NMK 63/1938
Gift, 1938

Chairs with wide, rounded backs and legs that curved well outwards, inspired by the klismos chairs of antiquity, were included in Louis Masreliez's furnishing of Gustav III's Pavilion at Haga. They were made in 1791 by Erik Öhrmark. The same form recurs on both gilded and painted chairs in the following decades.

The Empire – the Age of Karl XIV Johan

THE EMPIRE STYLE COVERS a period which in Sweden stretches from around 1800 to the beginning of the 1840s. It coincides for the most part with the reign of the first of the Bernadotte monarchs, who came to Sweden as Crown Prince in 1810. In 1818 he ascended the throne as Karl XIV Johan and lived until 1844, the year which is generally regarded as the end of the Empire, the Age of Karl Johan (Karl Johanstiden) as it is more commonly known in Sweden.

This era saw the transition from an old society in stagnation to a thrusting new industrial society. Finland had been ceded to Russia in 1809, but Sweden then entered into union with Norway in 1814. Karl XIV Johan showed a considerable talent for politics as he successfully led Sweden into the industrial age, and this former warrior in Napoleon's army strove hard to keep Sweden in a constant state of peace.

At the end of the 1820s Karl Johan built Rosendal, the small pleasure palace in Royal Djurgården in Stockholm. The palace was built and furnished in the French Empire style, with dark mahogany furniture, textiles in strong colours with distinct patterns, porphyry vases from Älvdalen and an abundance of bronze objects, both Swedish and French.

Despite such favourable conditions the French Empire style did not become widespread in Sweden. It was best represented among the royals and the aristocracy, but also appeared in the homes of the middle classes with a simpler, more Swedish flavour where it remained until the 1840s. In the manor houses, vicarages and bourgeois homes the Empire was adapted to meet the functional needs of daily life rather than those of ceremonial entertainment.

JAN VON GERBER

Urn, 1820s/30s
Porphyry with French bronzes
Älvdalen Porphyry Factory,
Älvdalen
H 63
NMK 26/1907
Gift, 1907

Karl XIV Johan personally owned Älvdalen Porphyry Factory. Porphyry, a rare stone, was greatly treasured during the Empire. The King gave porphyry objects as gifts and also ran an organised trade via agents in Paris, often receiving payment in the form of gilt bronzes.

Armchair, c. 1800
Painted wood, upholstery 1930s
Ephraim Ståhl, chair-maker in Stockholm 1794–1820
H 79
NMK 126/1983
Purchase, 1983

This elegant chair shows the unadulterated classicised style of the Empire. With its outwardly curved legs it can be seen as a free interpretation of the Greek klismos chair.

Chair, early 19th century
Painted wood, with pastellage decoration, upholstery later
Unmarked
H 86
NMH 62/1937
Purchase, 1937

After Napoleon's campaign in Egypt in 1798 the classicised style was complemented by Egyptian motifs. The front legs and back uprights of this Swedish chair were inspired by the Egyptian lotus columns.

Chair, 1830s
Polished beech, latticed cane
Unmarked
H 80.5
NMK 55/1990
Purchase, 1990

The echoes of the grand Empire style were lighter, both in colour and in form. Lighter indigenous woods replaced mahogany. This chair represents this later stage of development through its airily composed back and its latticed cane seat.

Interior from Såtenäs House, 1830s
Watercolour and washed pencil drawing
Lars Wilhelm Kylberg (1798–1865)
15.2 x 18.8
NMH 645/1892
Gift, 1892

Såtenäs House was owned by Kylberg, a soldier and illustrator. Here he is demonstrating his artwork for a close friend. The room is furnished with light birch furniture positioned along the walls. Only the light chairs move. The curtain arrangements are Empire style, and appear modern even in an interior that was now decorated in an otherwise simpler style.

Mirror and Table, 1815–20
Gilded wood, white marble
Stockholm
H 190 and H 78
NMK 42–43/1990
Purchase, 1990

The mirror and accompanying richly gilded table show the Empire style's emphasis on splendour. The powerfully modelled, lunette-shaped top-piece, the winged griffon and the fasces are all recurring, familiar elements in this period.

Medallion and Busts Karl XIV Johan and Oscar I, 1820s/30s
Cast iron
Unmarked
Finspångs bruk
D 10 (medallion)
H 16.5 (busts)
NMK 49/1991, NMK 40–41/1990
Purchases, 1991 and 1990

The success of the production of cast iron ornaments and jewellery in Berlin inspired an equivalent production in Sweden – the country of iron. Finspångs bruk was successful with its production of smaller objects such as clock stands, candlesticks, inkstands and statuettes.

Hanging Ceiling Lamp, 1820s/30s
Gilded and patinated bronze
Stockholm
H 74
NMK 38/1889
Purchase, 1889

This ceiling lamp in the form of an antique oil lamp is one of several variations made at this time in the Stockholm workshops. This model was obviously popular judging by the relatively large number which have been preserved.

Chair and Table, 1830s
Mahogany with stencilled decoration, cover of green silk damask
H 87.5 and H 80.5
NMK 33 and 19/1990
Purchase, 1990

The bourgeoisie in the time of Karl Johan often had furniture made of birch, stained in imitation of mahogany. Bronze mountings were replaced by thin pressed brass mountings or stencilling. The chair with its simple, clear lines, outward-curving legs, and shield-shaped back is the most common at this time. The Imperial style had become bourgeois.

Romanticism and Historicism

WITH THE FALL OF NAPOLEON the Empire style lost its appeal, as the war-ravaged countries of Europe associated it with a dominant power which had finally been broken. The ensuing period was characterised by a transfer of power from the princes to the citizens of the towns and cities. In tandem with the political changes the Biedermeier style grew up in the German-speaking countries, where France's leading role was taken over by England which now set the trends technologically and in the decorative arts. In the absence of a naturally developed style, there was a search through history for a style based on a romantic flight from reality towards other countries and other times. In the mid-18th century the English were already showing an interest in the Gothic.

In Sweden the stiff Empire style gave way to softer forms around 1830. The late Empire period, in the 1830s and 1840s, was the real Biedermeier period in Sweden. Light woods and naturalistic floral designs were mixed with softer Empire forms in mahogany. The furniture is given a practical form with sparse ornamentation against light, smooth surfaces of birch, maple and other woods. Popular motifs are portraits, townscapes and interiors, expressing an interest in the immediate environment.

Woven linen damask textiles remained an exclusive craft in the beginning of the 19th century, requiring special looms and specially trained weavers. The biggest factory, apart from Flor, was Vadstena, established in 1752. In the 1790s work began to be marked with the name in capital letters and the loom number. In the early 1800s the factory flourished as damask linen became more widespread. Besides long tablecloths and napkins, square 'tea cloths' were woven for smaller tables.

Flintware and transfer printing brought about a rapid development of the ceramics industry in the 19th century. Gustavsberg factory on Värmdö was set up in 1825. Both there and at Rörstrand models and patterns came at first from England, but soon Swedish architecture and landscapes were regarded as interesting motifs for decoration. This was facilitated by the upswing in their pictorial reproduction at this time, with such works as *Sweden – Far and Near* by Ulrik Tersner (1779–1828) and *Album Pittoresque* by Carl Johan Billmark (1804–70) providing visual models.

The neo-Gothic reached Sweden at this period, sometimes referred to as Geatish or Oscar I style. It gained a certain grip through interest in Swedish history which Geaticism/Gothicism represented. This nationalist focus was vigorously pursued by Karl XIV Johan and Oscar I. As Crown Prince, Oscar I instituted a neo-Gothic Room in the Royal Palace in Stockholm.

The only 19th-century style that can be considered purely national is the old Norse dragon style (a.k.a. Viking Revival), current in the 1870s, and linked to advances in archaeological research. Within decorative art it was exploited mainly by August Malmström (1829–1901), the architect Magnus Isaeus (1841–90) and the textile artist Hanna Winge (1836–96).

The 19th century was also the age of exhibitions, as industry needed to show off its new developments. The 1823 Stockholm Exhibition was at first a modest affair. The world exhibitions in Europe and the USA were key sources of inspiration, but led to conformity in production and ideas.

BARBRO HOVSTADIUS

Drawing Room Furniture from Wallox-Säby House, 1830s
Polished birch, printed cotton (not original)
H 93.5, H 102
NMK 39–40/1991
Purchase, 1991

A complete set of furniture with the same material, colour, decoration, and upholstery was an innovation at this time. This set consists of two mirrors with console table, two three-piece suites with oval tables, armchairs and a rocking chair. The freely grouped furniture was originally placed in a room with stencil-painted floor and floral wallpaper.

Dinner Service, 1840s
Flintware, with *Black Sweden* (*Svart Sverige*)
printed decoration
Rörstrand Porcelain Factory, Stockholm
H 25.5 (tureen) and L 47.5 (meat dish)
NMK 178/1902
NMK 60–62/1991
NMK 25/1971
NMK 4/1992
Purchases, 1902, 1991, 1971 and 1992.

Services decorated in the *Black Sweden* style appeared in the 1840s and continued to be made for a couple of decades. The royal palaces are represented along with well-known historic sites.

Tablecloth, 1830s
Linen damask
Vadstena Damask Factory,
190 x 146.5
NMK 95/1991
Purchase, 1991

The pattern showing Vadstena Palace surrounded by women grouped in pairs to symbolise Sweden and Norway and the border of trophies was one of the innovations which came out of the Vadstena factory in the 1830s. It was inspired by German damasks with romantic images.

52 ■ A SWEDISH LEGACY

Portrait of Oscar I, 1846

Black and white silk
Lars Gabriel Horngren (1817–81)
K.A. Almgren silk weavers,
Stockholm 1833–1974, 1993–
48 x 40.5
NMK 84/1955
Gift, 1955

The portrait of King Oscar I woven in silk was a common decoration in mid-19th-century homes. Following his studies in Lyons, silk weaver K.A. Almgren introduced the first jacquard loom into Sweden in c. 1830.

Coffee Pot, 1860

Silver, chased and moulded
Gustav Möllenborg & Co,
Stockholm 1860–1930
H 26.3
NMK 4/1972
Purchase, 1972

This coffee pot shows how new rococo and naturalism were mixed, the pot's smooth silver surface setting off the roughness of the handle's vine with leaf and grape clusters.

ROMANTICISM AND HISTORICISM

Tablecloth, 1873
Broadcloth with relief seam
125 x 125
NMK 706/1885
Gift from Swedish Society for
Industrial Design, 1884

The pattern was designed by Agnes Rijswijk, a student of August Malmström, and embroidered by Anna Fleetwood from instructions by Hanna Winge. The cloth was among the work shown at the world exhibition in Vienna in 1873. The view was expressed in the Swedish press that the patterns demonstrated the richness of old Norse art and did not need to copy foreign models.

Chair, 1882

Ebony, pearwood, ivory and marble inlay
Magnus Isaeus (1841–90)
Carl P. Svensson, upholsterer to the Royal Court, Stockholm
H 130.5
NMK 147/1891
Gift from Lars Olof Smith, 1891

The chair was a part of the set of furniture commissioned by the well-to-do Lars O. Smith, 'king of schnapps', creator of the Absolut brand of Swedish vodka. This magnificent neo-renaissance piece is embellished with female figures wearing traditional costume from the Skåne region. Smith was born in Skåne in southern Sweden, and the schnapps which made his fortune came from distilleries in Skåne and neighbouring Blekinge.

Teapot and Sauce Dish, 1877

Flintware with Nordic Style painted decoration
Daniel Johan Carlsson
Gustavsberg Porcelain Factory, Stockholm
H 22 and H 18.5
NMK 1974, 1976/1885
Gift from Swedish Society for Industrial Design, 1884

A number of services were made at Gustavsberg in Nordic Style, with dragon arabesques taken from runestones. This example was designed by D.J. Carlsson, the first of the students at the vocational Tekniska skolan, later Konstfackskolan, who became a professional pattern designer for the industrial arts.

From the Turn of the Century to Swedish Grace

THE INTERNATIONAL JUGENDSTIL reached Sweden via the foreign travels of artists, publications, and the great exhibitions of art and industry. Artists first went for the flowing organic lines and curves of, for example, plants, flowers and waves, then later for sparse geometrical design.

The Modern movement as it became known was shaped in Sweden as elsewhere by a group of artists and architects who were also interested in practical art. Prior to the Stockholm Exhibition of 1897 the painters Alf Wallander and Gunnar Wennerberg were taken on at the ceramic factories, Rörstrand and Gustavsberg. The renewal they brought about also led to work for the glass industry dominated by Kosta and Reijmyre. Artistic design of furniture became the concern of architects such as Ferdinand Boberg, Carl Westman and Carl Bergsten and the painter J.A.G. Acke.

The period 1890–1914 is a flourishing chapter in the history of Swedish textile art. The oldest of the textile workshops in production was the Friends of Textile Art Association, established in 1874. Its aim was to manage the cultural heritage and the traditional techniques and patterns of Swedish textiles. The same applied to the Swedish Handicraft Society, the Swedish Industrial Art Exhibition Selma Giöbel, and Thyra Grafström's textile workshop. The (mostly female) artists who began work in the 1880s and 1890s became the leading figures in textile art.

The social dimension within the aesthetic movement of the period was most clearly expressed by the authoress Ellen Key (1849–1926) particularly in the booklet *Beauty for All* in 1899. A concrete inspiration for Key were Carl Larsson's paintings of his own house in Sundborn, a house which was radical in its simplicity and filled with happy colours and home comforts.

After the Baltic Exhibition in Malmö in 1914, industrial art from the Baltic countries (featured at the exhibition) was heavily criticised at home for being stagnant and mannered. Only the textile art had received praise. The Swedish Society for Industrial Design was founded in 1845 to improve design standards in everyday life. Erik Wettergren (1883–1961) formulated a programme, taking older work from the 18th century as the model. At the same time Gregor Paulsson (1889–1977), Elsa Gullberg (1886–1984) and others had become familiar with the Deutscher Werkbund movement and the ideas behind functionalism. An office was set up to facilitate contact between artists and industry, and results were shown at the Exhibition of the Home in 1917. The socialist goals were not met, the products being too expensive for the general public, but a series of young architects and designers arrived on the scene and were taken on within industry. Including Simon Gate and Edvard Hald at Orrefors, Edvin Ollers at Kosta and Wilhelm Kåge at Gustavsberg, these designers led Swedish decorative art and design to decades of international success.

Building work on Stockholm City Hall was completed in 1923. Importantly the interior provided work for many artists. The style is a combination of national–romanticism and classicism. Swedish 1920s classicism made its breakthrough at the Paris World Exhibition in 1925. Expressive yet graceful it was seen as typically Swedish and dubbed Swedish Grace by the English critic, Morton Shand.

BARBRO HOVSTADIUS

Poster for Stockholm Exhibition, 1897
Colour lithograph
Richard Bergh (1858–1919)
90 x 65
NMG 10/1936
Gift, 1898

Artistic posters were an innovation at the turn of the century. The painter Richard Bergh has captured the age's belief in the future in the Jugendstil arabesques and the billowing streamers.

Tapestry, *Skator i äppelträd (Magpies in Apple Tree)*, 1897
Alf Wallander (1862–1914)
Swedish Industrial Art Exhibition
S. Giöbel
335 x 59
NMK 95/1897
Purchase, Stockholm Exhibition, 1897

Decorative Vase, 1897
Porcelain
Alf Wallander (1862–1914)
Rörstrand Porcelain Factory, Stockholm
H 50
NMK 12/1897
Purchase, Stockholm Exhibition, 1897

The magpies in the tree are a national motif of the time. The vase was thrown and painted by Wallander, whose decoration often contains a sculpted element and fits the form well. The long, thin kakemono-like shape of the tapestry shows how Japanese inspiration and national motifs are mixed.

Vase,
1901
Porcelain
Alf Wallander (1862–1914)
Rörstrand Porcelain Factory,
Stockholm
H 31.5
NMK 882/1927
Gift from the maker, 1927

Delicate modelling and the suggestive, diffuse character of the underglaze painting enable the artist to achieve effects in keeping with the international Jugendstil.

Plates, *Gullviva and Liljekonvalje (Cowslip and Lily of the Valley)*, 1897
Bone china, with hand-painted decoration
Gunnar Wennerberg (1863–1914)
Gustavsberg Porcelain Factory, Stockholm
D 22
NMK 120–121/1966
Gift from the maker, 1966

Wennerberg's tableware with flower motif was displayed at the 1897 exhibition. His light stylising and natural colours pay tender homage to the Swedish flora.

Vase, 1897
Flintware
Gunnar Wennerberg (1863–1914)
Gustavsberg Porcelain Factory, Stockholm
H 20.5
NMK 28/ 1897
Purchase, Stockholm Exhibition, 1897

Wennerberg was a skilful flower painter who with ease transferred his motifs to three dimensional ceramics.

Book Cover, *Maskros (Dandelion)*, 1900
Paper
Arthur Sjögren (1874–1951)
AB Ljus förlag, Stockholm
NMK 148/1944
Purchased from the artist, 1944

Book Art underwent rapid modernisation at the turn of the century. The artist Arthur Sjögren pioneered paper sleeves to cover a bound book, this example being a collection of his own poetry.

Bowl, 1900
Cameo glass
Gunnar Wennerberg (1863–1914)
Kosta Glassworks, Kosta
H 12.5
NMK 6/1901
Gift from the maker, 1901

This dish was made for the World Exhibition in Paris in 1900. The artist was chosen to design glass in the spirit of Emile Gallé. He created a long series of motifs where he shows a humble relationship to the plants and flowers featured on the glass. The leaves on this dish are highly naturalistic and, in comparison to French glass from the same period, very Swedish.

Bowl with Lid, *Dansen (The Dance)*, 1903
Pewter
Aron Jerndahl (1858–1936)
Fabriks AB Herkules, Stockholm
H 17
NMK 115/1970
Gift, 1970

The soft pewter seems to take the shape of the peasant motif in a rhythmic, swirling dance. This bowl was greatly admired at this period for its artistic quality.

Dining Room Furniture, 1900
Oak
J.A.G. Acke (1859–1924)
Carl Johansson's Möbleringsaffär, Stockholm
H 75 (table)
NMK 78–82/1949
Gift, 1949

The painter and sculptor J.A.G. Acke did not design much furniture, but his work showed great artistic expression, with the form dominating the material.

Cupboard, 1909
Mahogany with intarsia
Ferdinand Boberg (1860–1946)
Nordiska Kompaniet (NK) workshops, Nyköping
H 204
NMK 6/1909
Gift, 1909

The architect Boberg was seeking a new style which did not imitate older forms. Through juxtaposition of concave and convex he allows the material to come into its own in a simple and refined fashion.

Tapestry, *Vårvinter (Spring/winter)*, 1907
Gustaf Fjaestad (1868–1948)
Maja Fjaestad (1873–1961)
143 x 267
NMK 280/1907
Purchase, 1907

It was Maja Fjaestad who persuaded her husband, the painter Gustaf Fjaestad, to make designs for textiles from his snow-covered landscapes. She and her sister would then weave in tapestry or knotted pile fabric. They formed an artists' collective called Rackstadgruppen by Racken lake in Värmland.

Tapestry, *Yggdrasil*, 1906
Gunnar Hallström (1875–1943)
Friends of Textile Art Association, Stockholm
335 x 148
NMK 78/1961
Purchase, 1961

The tapestry's national-romantic motif stems from the artist's interest in Viking archaeology. It made a strong impression on the author August Strindberg (1849–1912) who saw in it an illustration for his *Dream Play (Drömspelet)* in 1902.

Armchair, 1915

Walnut with cane seat
Carl Malmsten (1888–1972)
Carl Malmsten's workshop,
Stockholm
H 84.5
NMK 93/1957
Gift, 1957

With this chair Malmsten won a competition for the interior of Stockholm City Hall thus making his breakthrough as a leading furniture designer. He sought a new style of furniture based on historical heritage, this example taking the baroque as its starting point.

Jewel-case, *Heliga tre konungar (The Magi)*, 1914–16

Silver
Jacob Ängman (1876–1942)
Guldsmedsaktiebolaget (GAB), Stockholm
H 22
NMK 97/1928
Purchase, 1928

On the inside of the lid of this box with its medieval shape there is an elegant decoration in gold thread on purple velvet depicting the star of Bethlehem in a star-filled sky, framed by floral decoration. This is the most important work in Ängman's extensive repertoire.

Tapestry,
Enhörningen i skogen (The Unicorn in the Forest), 1917
Tapestry
Märta Måås-Fjetterström
(1873–1941)
Swedish Handicraft Society workshop, Vittsjö
225 x 128
NMK 34/1966
Purchase, 1966

History was the starting point for Märta Måås-Fjetterström, who became the leading exponent of modern Swedish textile art. Unable to weave herself she used the structure of the fabric when creating her stylised motifs for tapestries and knotted pile fabric rugs.

Urn, 1917
Graal glass, violet
Simon Gate (1883–1945)
Orrefors Glassworks, Orrefors
H 25
NMK 102/1957
Gift, 1957

The Graal technique took its name from the medieval legend of the Holy Grail, a vessel with a liquid shrouded with mystery in a clear glass. Cameo cutting is followed by further furnace work and then given a final clear casing. Sealing pictures in glass was an idea that the glassblower Knut Bergqvist had put into practice in 1915–16. When the artist Simon Gate was employed by the glassworks in 1916 he took on the challenge of developing this new technique. The Graal technique was a contributing factor in the rapid rise of Orrefors to being one of the most important glassworks in Sweden.

Sweet Jar, 1917
Blistered glass
(1888–1959)
Kosta Glassworks, Kosta
H 21
NMK 124/1960
Purchase, 1960

At the 1917 exhibition Kosta Glassworks showed a large number of objects designed by Edvin Ollers, a designer who they had recently employed. Inspired by earlier glasswork he produced drinking glasses and other objects in green or blue glass containing bubbles of air. The deliberately uneven quality was achieved by putting sand into the molten glass. The aim was to produce a simple, inexpensive glass, completely different to their sparkling crystal. The shapes are reminiscent of the baroque or, as in this case, 18th-century butter dishes.

Vase, *Triton*, 1917

Glass, dark violet colour
Simon Gate (1883–1945)
Orrefors Glassworks, Orrefors
H 22
NMK 177/1917
Purchase, 1917

These longitudinal, olive-cut facets, covering the whole of the vase, demonstrate a new cutting technique. It called for great skill not to spoil this decoration, the effect of which is wholly dependent on precision. Geometric forms like this are otherwise unusual at Orrefors.

Service, *Arbetarservisen (The Workers' Service)*, 1917

Flintware with printed Blue Lily decoration.
Wilhelm Kåge (1889–1960)
Gustavsberg Porcelain Factory, Stockholm
H 16 (pot)
NMK 22, 26, 27/1975, 125/1979
Purchases, 1975, and 1979

Kåge was the poster artist who became industrial art's greatest ceramic artist of the 20th century. The *workers' service* with its gently rounded 18th-century forms was his successful début at the Exhibition of the Home, 1917.

Chair, 1923
Stained and polished birch
Carl Hörvik (1882–1954), Stockholm
H 88
NMK 31/1988
Purchase, 1988

Modern classicism was trying to achieve a scaled-down simplicity, expressed here through simple construction and a spacious cane latticework.

Grandfather Clock, 1919
Jacaranda
Carl Malmsten (1888–1972)
Carl Malmsten's workshop, Stockholm
H 222
NMK 6/1920
Purchase, 1920

Malmsten was an important figure in the 1920s when ornamental furniture with intarsia decoration in 18th-century inspired classicism dominated furniture design.

Sample Tapestry, 1924
Linen, wool and gold thread
Einar Forseth (1892–1988)
Elsa Gullberg, Konserthuset's textile studio, Stockholm
136 x 187
NMK 136/1972
Purchase, 1972

The main auditorium in Stockholm Concert Hall was shaped like an ancient temple and painted in cold stone colours. Therefore Forseth's hangings for the balustrades were coloured purple, brick red and gold to give the space colour and splendour.

Bowl with lid, 1925
Flintware with painted decoration
Arthur Percy (1886–1976)
Gefle Porcelain Factory, Gävle
H 36
NMK 174/1930
Purchase, Stockholm Exhibition, 1930

This decorative punch bowl featuring a bacchante on the lid was first shown at the Paris Exhibition in 1925. With his ceramics Percy fulfilled the ambition of the age – to be both traditional and innovative.

FROM THE TURN OF THE CENTURY TO SWEDISH GRACE

Bowl, 1925
Glass, engraved decoration
Simon Gate (1883–1945)
Orrefors Glassworks, Orrefors
H 12
NMK 115/1966
Purchase, 1966

Swedish glass made its international breakthrough in Paris in 1925. Orrefors became a well-known name outside Sweden and received much high praise for its work including the engraved glass with classical decoration. There was nothing new in the technique itself, but the glass was valued for the clarity with which the artists worked. The fusion of form and decoration was also much admired. Orrefors now finally overtook Kosta in importance, becoming dubbed the Murano of the North.

DETAIL OF ENGRAVED DECORATION

Bowl with Lid, *Karusellskålen (The Carousel Dish)*, 1929
Glass, cut and engraved decoration
Ewald Dahlskog (1894–1950)
Kosta Glassworks, Kosta
H 38
NMK 262/1978
Purchase, 1978

The Carousel Dish is the best piece of cut glass that Ewald Dahlskog designed for Kosta. The figures move playfully on the cut and engraved crystal. Kosta wanted to renew the cutting technique as a way of competing with Orrefors engraved glass. This bowl with its thick walls heralds the heavy glasswork of the 1930s.

Vase, 1930
Stoneware with green glaze and silver decoration
Wilhelm Kåge (1889–1960)
Gustavsberg Porcelain Factory, Stockholm
H 26.5
NMK 180/1930
Purchase, Stockholm Exhibition, 1930

The silver decorated artwork, Argenta, invented by Kåge and introduced at the Stockholm Exhibition in 1930 was an expression of lingering classicism. There were a variety of decorations – dancing women, Japanese dragons and geometric designs. The green glaze was most common, though red was also used.

Sky Globe, 1929–30
Glass with engraved decoration, pewter stand
Edvard Hald (1883–1980)
Orrefors Glassworks, Orrefors
H 53
NMK 142/1930
Gift, 1930

This Sky Globe, with its rich and dense engraved decoration was one of the ornamental pieces that Orrefors made for the Stockholm Exhibition of 1930. It may be regarded as a magnificent close to the decade of engraved glass. Hald's spiritual interpretation of the heavens is accompanied by a modern ocean steamer.

From Functionalism to Scandinavian Design

THE STOCKHOLM EXHIBITION of 1930 made that year a milestone in 20th-century Swedish design. It was intended as a presentation of Swedish industrial art, handicraft and decorative art, which had met with such success in Paris in 1925. However, under the influence of Gregor Paulsson and radical young architects the focus was concentrated on the new functionalist ideas as seen in the architecture and interiors of homes. In white exhibition halls with glass facades, designed by the architect Gunnar Asplund, functionalism was displayed to the Swedish public for the first time, provoking strong feelings, both for and against. The new geometric lines were cold and harsh – tubular steel furniture, glass top tables, plain materials. But the industrially manufactured, functionally designed household articles met the demand for more attractive everyday objects. Ornamentation was anathema to the functionalists. Aesthetic expression came rather through the material and its practical application. Designers were happy to use bentwood, tubular steel and webbing, emphasising the techniques with textiles and the material with glass and ceramics. The value placed on these materials and the techniques led with time to a fruitful development for the decorative arts, which were able to achieve a freer form with the functional needs being realised differently.

The 1930s is the decade of exhibitions, both in Sweden and abroad. Participation in Expo Paris in 1937 and the New York World Exhibition in 1939 met with great success. The concept of Swedish Modern, a term coined by the English and American press, implied interiors with furniture of light woods and rounded shapes, and easy-care textiles with soft drapery and lively patterns in bright colours. Overall a new snug homeliness – furniture that was practical, unobtrusive and easy to live with.

The war interrupted international contacts. For the decorative arts this isolation meant a focus on individual creation, while industrial production was hampered by a shortage of material and labour. A series of exhibitions, at the Nationalmuseum among other places, focused on the relationship between industrial art and the hand-made creations of individual craftsmen. Housing problems were important during the 1940s and led to increased interest in industrially produced furniture textiles and household utensils. Hand-printed household textiles had been introduced in the 1930s and during the 1940s the textile industry began to engage Swedish artists as pattern designers. In parallel with mass production the glass and ceramic factories developed the production of hand-made, decorative objects. Bright, cheerful colours flourished.

In the mid-1950s Scandinavian decorative art and industrial design established a worldwide reputation when the Nordic countries together organised an exhibition, Design in Scandinavia. It was shown in 20 or more locations in the USA and Canada, making Scandinavian design an international concept.

BARBRO HOVSTADIUS

Armchair, 1931
Tubular steel and leather
Gunnar Asplund (1885–1940)
Nordiska Kompaniet, Stockholm
H 77
NMK 74/1966
Gift, 1966

Tubular steel furniture was one of the elements which shocked audiences at the Stockholm Exhibition, and was not accepted outside radical circles until the 1960s. Asplund's armchair with its pure, timeless form, designed for the board room of the Swedish Society for Industrial Design was, therefore, a lone example.

Rug, 1930
Hand-knotted wool pile fabric
Ingegerd Torhamn (1898–1994)
190 x 115
NMK 51/1967
Purchase, 1967

For artistic emphasis the progressive architects put rugs by the painter Ingegerd Torhamn in their interiors at the Stockholm Exhibition. Her inspiration for the abstract patterns and the subdued colours came from contemporary abstract painting.

Tea Caddy, 1930
Silver, ebony
Wiwen Nilsson, (1897–1974)
Wiwen Nilsson, Lund
H 15
NMK 171/1930
Purchase, Stockholm Exhibition, 1930

By around 1930 Wiwen Nilsson had developed the austere geometric style that he worked at with uncompromising consistency during his whole working life. The desired eggshell-silver surface was achieved by 'polishing' with finely sieved sand.

Vase, 1930
Earthenware, glazed
Ewald Dahlskog (1894–1950)
Boberg Faience Factory, Gävle
H 24.5
NMK 185/1930
Purchase, Stockholm Exhibition, 1930

The horizontal rings are formed from the ceramic material but at the same time they emphasise the spherical shape. This is a decorative design wholly in keeping with the aims of functionalism.

Vase, 1930
Glass with black foot
Simon Gate (1883–1945)
Orrefors Glassworks, Orrefors
H 24.5
NMK 195/1930
Purchase, Stockholm Exhibition, 1930

When Simon Gate designed this blown vase with bulbous sides he was inspired by the spirit of the age, with its pure, undecorated surfaces. The thickness of the glass produced new effects when the light was reflected in it. The choice of black for the foot and the rim was intended to emphasise the shape of the vase.

Bookbindings, 1930s

Morocco, gold embossed
Berta Svensson
Herzog & Sons, Stockholm
NMK 217/1930
Purchase, Stockholm Exhibition, 1930

Leather, gold embossed
Akke Kumlien (1884–1949)
P.A. Norstedt and Sons Bookbinders,
Stockholm
NMK 215/1931
Purchase, 1931

Morocco, gold embossed
Sven Erik Skawonius (1908–81)
N. Bernhard Andersson's Bookbinders,
Stockholm
NMK 35/1937
Purchase, Nyttokonst Exhibition, 1937

Interest in typography, layout and artistic bookbinding in the 1930s led to the establishment of the institution called Swedish Book Art (Svensk Bokkonst) in 1934, which awards prizes each year for the 25 best books.

Dish and Flower Glass, *Sio*, 1929–30

Crystal glass, yellow
Gerda Strömberg (1879–1952)
Eda Glassworks, Eda
D 40 (dish) and H 20 (flower glass)
NMK 200/1930, 28/1987
Purchase, Stockholm Exhibition, 1930, and purchase, 1987

Gerda Strömberg strove uncompromisingly for simplicity and purity. This was something new in the late 1920s and gave Eda Glassworks its own niche, and the shimmering hues set Eda apart from its competitors.

Magazine Shelves and Chair, 1930s

Light-stained ash
Axel B. Larsson (1898–1975)
AB Svenska Möbelfabrikerna, Bodafors
H 106 (rack) and H 80 (chair)
NMK 75–76/1934
Purchase, 1934

AB Svenska Möbelfabrikerna (Swedish Furniture Manufacturers), one of the largest furniture manufacturers in Sweden, was among the first to manufacture attractive 'mass-produced' furniture. Their principal designer up to 1956 was the architect Axel Larsson who in the 1930s worked in an elegant and refined functionalism.

Curtain, *Ladbrook Square*, 1937
Tapestry weft, picks inserted by hand
Märta Måås-Fjetterström (1873–1941)
Märta Måås-Fjetterström's workshop, Båstad
252 x 153
NMK 278/1940
Purchase, 1940

The drawing for this piece was based on the memory of a trip to London, where the image of a town with grey façades, high windows and smoking chimneys has been stylised into a decorative pattern.

Work Chair, 1934
Bentwood beech, latticed webbing
Bruno Mathsson (1907–88)
Karl Mathsson & Co, Värnamo
H 83
NMK 49/1959
Purchase, 1959

Bruno Mathsson had a long Swedish and international career after his début in 1936 – his solution to the 'mechanics of sitting' in bentwood and latticed webbing.

Fabric Print, *Spaljé (Trellis-work)*, 1936
Film printing on rayon
Arthur Percy (1886–1976)
AB Elsa Gullberg Textilier och Inredning, Stockholm
W 95
NMK 73/1992
Gift, 1992

The multi-talented artist Percy, painter, potter and glass designer, also designed patterns for fabric prints. Close, decorative flower motifs dominate, but in the 1930s he also produced some skilfully drawn compositions of a more abstract character.

Chest of Drawers, *Skåp med 21 lådor (Chest with 21 Drawers)*, c. 1938
Amboyna, walnut
Josef Frank (1885–1967)
Svenskt Tenn, Stockholm
H 120
NMK 32/1952
Purchase, 1952

Josef Frank designed several variations on the chest of drawers theme, inspired by both English and Asian furniture. Here he has created a balanced movement through an apparently random variation of shape and size in the drawers and handles.

Sculpture, *Pärlfiskarna (The Pearl Fishers)*, 1931
Engraved glass
Vicktor Lindstrand (1904–83)
Orrefors Glassworks, Orrefors
H 40
NMK 1/1971
Gift, 1971

The engraved pearl fishers move lithely through the water observed by an octopus. The form is a wholly integrated sculpture. The bulging shape, the thick glass, and the black foot were features that came to typify 1930s glassware.

Vase, 1939
Glass, Ariel technique
Edvin Öhrström (1906–94)
Orrefors Glassworks, Orrefors
H 18
NMK 1076/1939
Purchase, 1939

Ariel glass, with bubbles of air complementing the colours, is named after the air spirit in Shakespeare's *The Tempest*. The technique became most strongly associated with Öhrström who investigated its possibilities thoroughly. Motifs appear as trapped dreams, in this case the subject is an African princess.

Dish, 1934
Silver
Erik Fleming (1894–1954)
Guldsmedsaktiebolaget (GAB), Stockholm
H 9
NMK 130/1934
Gift from the maker, 1934

Erik Fleming, with his company Ateljé Borgila, was a leading silversmith, known for his craftsmanship in a measured classicism. Briefly in the 1930s he designed models for GAB for serial production on a larger scale.

Jug and Plate from the Christina service, 1943
Flintware, painted and printed decoration
Arthur Percy (1886–1976)
Gefle Porcelain Factory, Gävle
H 15.5 (jug), D 25.5 (plate)
NMK 87–88/1943
Gift from the maker, 1943

The model for the service is the same as Percy's Blue Vine, 1939, but the Christina decorative motif was named after Princess Christina who was born in 1943. A yellow butterfly links the motif to the Palace of Haga in Stockholm where the Crown Prince's family lived.

Vase, *Komedianter i regn (Strolling Players in the Rain)*, 1944
Flintware
Stig Lindberg (1916–82)
Gustavsberg Porcelain Factory, Stockholm
H 28.5
NMK 24/1944
Purchase, 1944

Only individual, hand-made pieces were created at the Gustavsberg Studio. Wilhelm Kåge and Stig Lindberg worked there with faiences and flintware painted with overglaze colour, which gave them great freedom. Lindberg here gives his playful imagination a melancholic touch by allowing the colours to run slightly.

Cigarette Box, 1942
Silver with gold inlay
Sven Arne Gillgren (1913–92)
Guldsmedsaktiebolaget (GAB), Stockholm
H 10
NMK 217/1942
Gift, 1942

In a number of boxes with lids from the 1940s Gillgren worked with naturalistic decoration and African motifs on geometric-shaped containers with geometric shapes. These were personally inspired art pieces, produced alongside a large production of secular and religious silver made at GAB, where Gillgren was artistic director.

Rug, *Snäckorna (The Shells)*, 1943
Tapestry
Barbro Nilsson (1899–1983)
AB Märta Måås-Fjetterström, Båstad
190 x 170
NMK 41/1947
Purchase, 1947

In 1942 Barbro Nilsson became administrative and artistic director of Märta Måås-Fjetterström's workshop, after the latter died. In the first few years she quickly renewed 'carpet art' by using the tapestry technique for a series of carpets with sea and berry motifs. She was well grounded in the technical aspects, and she worked directly at the loom, where the compositions came out of a close interplay of the technique and her own sketches.

Draft Design for Interior, 1946
Drawing with fabric samples
Elsa Gullberg (1886–1984)
AB Elsa Gullberg Textilier och
Inredning, Stockholm
29 x 23
NMK 177/1996
Gift from Friends of the
Nationalmuseum, 1996

This interior, with its mass-produced yet artistically designed furniture and well-matched textiles in bright colours, illustrates the concept of Swedish Modern. Elsa Gullberg herself designed many of the textiles which her company produced. She was creatively influential in the field of practical textiles, both hand-woven and machine-made.

Chair, 1944
Bentwood, compression-moulded mahogany veneer
Carl-Axel Acking (b. 1910)
AB Svenska Möblefabrikerna, Bodafors
H 79
NMK 22/ 1955
Gift, 1955

Acking's award-winning easy-assembly chair with bentwood framework and compression-moulded seat and back was an advanced piece of factory-made furniture.

Cabinet, *Livets vågskål (The Scales of Life)*, 1950
Erik Chambert (1902–88)
AB Chambert Furniture Factory,
Norrköping
H 132
NMK 1/1989
Gift bequeathed by the artist, 1989

For designs for intarsia on furniture, cloth prints and wall hangings, furniture designer Erik Chambert turned to his constructivist pictures. This was his contribution to a bringing together of free art and craftwork, which gave decorative expression new intrinsic value within 'utility' art.

Curtain, *Manhattan*, 1953
Double weave
Ingrid Dessau (b.1923)
150 x 238
NMK 120/1957
Gift, 1957

Ingrid Dessau's fabrics from the 1950s were created at the loom in an interplay between technique and motif. Knowledge of her field, and an interesting use of colours caused her to be regarded, early in her career, as one of the foremost textile artists.

Vase, *Nät på tork (Nets Drying)*, 1951
Engraved glass
Vicke (Viktor) Lindstrand
(1904–83)
Kosta Glassworks, Kosta
H 33
NMK 26 /1954
Gift, 1954

The drying nets motif has been cleverly used with fine lines running over the whole vase, exploiting with great finesse the transparency of the glass. Lindstrand strove constantly to create new magic with glass. Nothing was impossible.

Vase and Glass with Feet,
Tulip Glass, 1954
Nils Landberg (1907–91)
Orrefors Glassworks, Orrefors
H 51.5 (vase) H 39 (glass)
NMK 48/1985, 173/1989
Purchase, 1985;
gift from the artist, 1989

The tulip glasses have often been used to illustrate 1950s form. The beautiful contours and the subdued colours are in keeping with the times. The glasses placed great demands on the blowers, especially when the artist wanted to draw out the glass to breaking point.

Candlesticks, 1954

Silver
Sigurd Persson (b. 1914)
Sigurd Persson. Atelier för
Ädelsmide, Stockholm
H 19.5
NMK 28–29/1958
Gift, 1958

Organic growth is a key element in Sigurd Persson's creative process alongside geometric form, which gives a fixed, austere starting point.

Vase, 1954

Stoneware with blue-grey glaze
Berndt Friberg (1899–1981)
Gustavsberg Porcelain Factory,
Stockholm
H 16.5
NMK 2/1954
Purchase, 1954

Berndt Friberg was a very skilful turner who, in addition to his work under Wilhelm Kåge, developed into a stoneware artist in his own right. Drawing on the Far East, he shaped heavy closed vases covered in glazes with silken matt surfaces and soft-coloured, so-called 'hare's fur'.

Pieces of Service, *Blåeld (Blue Fire)*, 1950
Glazed flintware
Herta Bengtsson (1917–93)
Rörstrand Porcelain Factory, Stockholm
H 10.5 (vegetable dish), D 20.5 (Bowl),
H 22 (jug)
NMK 72–73/1973
Gift from the maker, 1973

This service became a minor sensation with its organic and lightly asymmetrical shapes and its brilliant blue colour. It was designed for the new homeowner who would buy individual pieces as he or she needed them. The colour scheme was well planned, with pieces used for drinking or eating in white, and serving vessels in blue.

Serving Vessels, *Picknick (Picnic)*, 1956
China with printed and painted decoration
Marianne Westman (b. 1928)
Rörstrand Porcelain Factory, Stockholm
H 14–22
NMK 72–75, 77/1955
Purchase, 1955

Artistically designed and industrially manufactured utensils were characterised by well-coordinated forms and cheerful decoration. Design had become a respectable word.

Vases,
1954 and 1957
Glass with added decoration
Erik Höglund (1932–98)
Boda Glassworks, Boda
H 37, 17.5
NMK 47/1954, 83/1972
Gifts from the maker, 1954, 1972

Erik Höglund played with glass irreverently and unromantically. The strong shapes, often in blown glass with heavy decorations added, were a form of protest, a means of escaping from the elegant perfection that made Swedish glass famous. Nevertheless, his work always has a keen artistic base.

Telephones, *Ericofon*, 1950

Thermoplast
Gösta Thames (b. 1916)
Telefonaktiebolaget LM Ericsson
H 21, H 23.5
NMK 89/1974, 156/1976
Gifts from the maker, 1974 and 1976

Fabric Print, *Claro*, 1944

Cotton fabric
Astrid Sampe (b. 1909)
AB Ljungbergs textil tryck, Floda for NK's textile room.
W 120
NMK 32/1951
Gift from the maker, 1951

Ericofon, also called Kobran (the Cobra), was first introduced in 1953 and was the first telephone to have all its components in one piece. The cover was originally made in two parts (the white one) but in the new version (the red one) it was moulded whole. It was manufactured in six different colours.

Fabric, *Historieboken (The History Book)*, 1957

Double weave
Kaisa Melanton (b. 1920)
Friends of Textile Art Association, Stockholm
110 x 138
NMK 149/1960
Purchase, 1960

This fabric is part of a series of black and white compositions inspired by the random flashing images of the television screen. Kaisa Melanton is a multi-talented textile artist, whose images are often subtly critical of society.

Index

AB Chambert Furniture Factory, Norrköping 88
AB Elsa Gullberg Textilier och Inredning, Stockholm 81, 87
AB Ljungbergs Textiltryck, Floda 95
AB Ljus forlag 61
AB Märta Mååas-Fjetterström 86
AB Svenska Möbelfabrikerna, Bodafors 79, 87
Acke, J. A. G. 56, 63
Acking, Carl-Axel 87
Älvdalen Porphyry Factory 44
Ängman, Jacob 66
Årre, Olof 32
Asplund, Gunnar 74, 75

Bengtsson, Herta 92
Bergh, Richard 57
Bergs, Frantz 24
Bergsten, Carl 56
Bielke, Axel 9, 23, 30, 42
Billmark, Carl Johan 50
black Sweden style 52
Boberg, Ferdinand 56, 63
Boberg Faience Factory, Gävle 77
Boda Glassworks 94
Bucher, Paul de 14, 15

Carlsson, Daniel Johan 55
Caroline baroque style 14-20
Chambert, Erik 88
classicism, Swedish 56-73

Dahlskog, Ewald 72, 77
Dessau, Ingrid 89
Drenchler, Vieth Fijtsson 17

Eda Glassworks 79
Ehrensvärd, Carl August 40
Elstermann, Kristoffer 19
empire style 44-49
Ernst, Petter 23
Eskilsson, Nils 14

Fabriks AB Herkules, Stockholm 62
Falke, Jakob von 9
Finspångs bruk 48
Fjaestad, Gustaf 64
Fjaestad, Maja 64
Fleetwood, Anna 54
Fleming, Erik 83
Floberg, Arvid 41
Flor Linen Mill 24, 50
Forseth, Einar 71
Frank, Josef 81
Frantzen, Johan Otto 33
Friberg, Berndt 91
Fridsberg, Olof 26
Friends of Textile Art Association 95
functionalism 56, 74-95

Gate, Simon 56, 68, 69, 72, 77
Gefle Porcelain Factory, Gävle 71, 84
Gillgren, Sven Arne 86
Gothenburg Glassworks 40
graal technique 68
Guldsmedsaktiebolaget (GAB), Stockholm 66, 83, 86
Gullberg, Elsa 56, 71, 87
Gustav Möllenborg & Co 53
Gustavsberg Porcelain Factory 50, 55, 56, 60, 69, 73, 85, 91

Hald, Edvard 56, 73
Hallström, Gunnar 65
Hårleman, Carl 20, 21, 25
Hasselquist, Olaus 31
Haupt, Georg 37, 39
Hedberg, Johan 23
Herzog & Sons, Stockholm 78
Höglund, Erik 94
Horngren, Lars Gabriel 53
Horvik, Carl 70

Isaeus, Magnus 50, 55

Jerndahl, Aron 62
Johansson, Carl 63
Johansson, Johan 17
Jugendstil, international 56-73

K.A. Almgren 53
Kåge, Wilhelm 56, 69, 73, 85, 91
Karl Mathsson & Co, Värnamo 80
Kelson, Kilian 34
Key, Ellen 56
Konserthuset's textile studio 71
Kosta Glassworks 20, 56, 61, 68, 72, 90
Kumlien, Akke 78
Kungsholm Glassworks 14, 19
Kylberg, Lars Wilhelm 47

Landberg, Nils 90
Larsson, Axel B. 79
Larsson, Carl 56
Lindberg, Stig 85
Lindstrand, Vicktor 82, 90
Ljung, Pehr 43

Mååas-Fjetterström, Märta 67, 80
Malmsten, Carl 66, 70
Malmström, August 50, 54
Marieberg Faience Factory 8, 9, 20, 27, 31, 32, 33, 42
Martin, Olof 22
Masreliez, Adrien 32, 37
Masreliez, Louis 36, 43
Mathsson, Bruno 80
Melanton, Kaisa 95

N. Bernhard Andersson's Bookbinders 78
neo-classicism 36-43
neo-gothic style (Geatish or Oscar I style) 50
Nilsson, Barbro 86
Nilsson, Wiwen 76
Nordic style 50, 55
Nordin, Lars 25
Nordiska Kompaniet (NK) 63, 75
Nützel, Johan 16

Öhrmark, Erik 43
Öhrström, Edvin 83
Ollers, Edvin 56, 68
Orrefors Glassworks 56, 68, 69, 72, 73, 77, 82, 83, 90

P.A. Norstedt & Sons 78
Paulsson, Gregor 56, 74
Percy, Arthur 71, 81, 84
Persson, Sigurd 91
Petri, Henning 16
Precht, Christian 23

Rehn, Jean Eric 22, 30, 36, 37, 38, 39
Reijmyre Glassworks 56
Rijswijk, Agnes 54
rococo style 20-35
Rörstrand Porcelain Factory 8, 9, 20, 22, 23, 27, 30, 31, 50, 52, 56, 58, 59, 92
Ryberg, Simsom 35, 40

Sampe, Astrid 95
Schalin, Carl 28
Schnack, Peter 23
Scholander, Fredrik Wilhelm 8, 9
Sjögren, Arthur 61
Skawonius, Sven Erik 78
Stafhell, Gustaf, the Elder 21
Ståhl, Ephraim 46
Sten, Henrik 42
Stockholms Manufabrique 23
Strindberg, August 65
Strömbäck Glassworks, Umea 40
Strömberg, Gerda 79
Stüler, Friedrich August 8
Sundberg, Eric 29
Svenskt Tenn, Stockholm 81
Svensson, Berta 78
Svensson, Carl P. 55

Swedish Handicraft Society, Vittsjö 56, 67

Telefonaktiebolaget LM Ericsson 95
Tersner, Ulrik 50
Tessin, Nicodemus, the Younger 14
Thames, Gösta 95
Torhamn, Ingegerd 76
Trautzell, Abraham 16

Vadstena Damask Factory 50, 52
Vasa renaissance style 14-19
Västerås School 14

Wahlberg, Erik 31
Wallander, Alf 56, 58, 59
Wennerberg, Gunnar 56, 60, 61
Westman, Marianne 93
Westman, Carl 56
Wettergren, Erik 56
Winge, Hanna 50, 54

Zethelius, Pehr 35, 42

NK 995 .S93 1998

A Swedish legacy